THE USBORNE
ROUND THE WORLD
COOKBOOK

Caroline Young

Designed by Carol Law

Illustrated by Nadine Wickenden

**Additional illustrations by Barry Jones
and Annabel Spenceley**

Cookery consultant: Sarah Barrass
With special thanks to Julia Kirby-Jones

Food around the world

This book takes you on a worldwide tour of food, cooking and eating traditions. You will find out how to make some of the world's most famous dishes for yourself and how to serve them in the local style. The list below tells you which recipes from each country are in the book. The stars on the map show where the countries are.

Canada

 1 **US**
Pages 6-7
Pancakes
Hamburgers
Banana milkshake

US

2 **Latin (South) America**
Pages 8-9
Refried beans
Guacamole
Tacos
Tomato salsa

Caribbean

3 **Caribbean**
Pages 10-11
Mango ice cream
Banana bread

4 **Africa**
Pages 12-13
Peanut bread
Bobotie

5 **Spain and Portugal**
Pages 14-15
Gazpacho
Sardine salad
Paella

South America

6 **France**
Pages 16-17
Salade niçoise
French apple tart

7 **The British Isles**
Pages 18-19
Irish stew
Scones

8 **Italy**
Pages 20-21
Pizza Margherita
Spaghetti Bolognese

9 **The Netherlands**
Pages 22-23
Cauliflower in cheese sauce
Fruit tarts

10 **Germany**
Pages 24-25
'Heaven and Earth'
Lebkuchen

11 **Central Europe**
Pages 26-27
Hungarian goulash
Dumplings
Sachertorte

12 **Scandinavia**
Pages 28-30
Smörgåsbord
Jansson's temptation
Red fruit pudding
Poor knights
Smørrebrød

13 **Switzerland**
Page 31
Raclette
Muesli

14 **Greece and Turkey**
Pages 32-33
Shish kebabs
Moussaka

15 **Middle East**
Pages 34-35
Homous
Tabouli
Halva

16 **Russia**
Pages 36-37
Russian salad
Beef Stroganoff

17 **China**
Pages 38-39
Sweet and sour spare ribs
Fried rice with vegetables

18 **India**
Pages 40-41
Bhuna gosht
Dhal
Cucumber raita

19 **Japan**
Pages 42-43
Vegetable casserole
Dipping sauce

20 **Indonesia**
Page 44
Chicken in coconut sauce

21 **Australia and New Zealand**
Page 45
Lamingtons

Jewish cooking
Pages 46-47
Cheesecake
Potato latkes

2

Scandinavia

12

7

Russia

9

10

16

Europe

11

13

6

5

8

14

Middle East

15

China

Japan

17

19

India

18

Africa

4

Indonesia

20

Australia

21

New Zealand

Why people eat what they eat

What people cook and eat around the world
depends on several things.

The weather in different places
affects which crops farmers
grow. The ones they grow most
are the cheapest to buy locally.
A country's traditional dishes
are usually made with these
local foods.

*Coconuts grow
well in
Indonesia, so are
used in many
local dishes.*

In some poor countries, if the weather
spoils the main crop, people have no
food. They may starve unless richer
countries can send some.

Wealthy countries can afford to buy
foods from all over the world. There
are many more different things for
people to choose to eat.

*Exotic fruit and vegetables
from the Caribbean or
Africa are found in US
grocery stores.*

Some people
choose not to eat
certain things.
Vegetarians do not
eat meat and vegans
don't eat meat, fish or
dairy foods (butter,
cheese and so on).
A religion may
forbid certain
things. Muslims and
Jews do not eat
pork, for example.

3

Before you start

The tips and hints on this page will help you enjoy your cooking and make sure you get the very best results. Read them all the way through before you start.

First of all

Before you try any recipe in this book, read it right through. If there's anything you don't understand, ask. Then do these things before you start.

Wash your hands well, tie back long hair and put on an apron.

Make sure the kitchen surfaces are clean and clear.

If you're told to, turn the oven on. For a fan oven (convection), reduce the heat as the manual says.

Get all the ingredients you will need measured out.

Wash any fruit and vegetables thoroughly in cold water.

Put an oven shelf in the right place:
Over 190°C (375°F)/Gas mark 5 – high
Over 160°C (325°F)/Gas mark 3 – middle
Below this temperature – low
Put it anywhere in a fan oven.

Safety first

Some things you do when you cook can be dangerous. Always follow these simple rules in the kitchen.

● Never start cooking without an adult in the kitchen.

● When you see this symbol in the book, take extra care.

● Be very careful when slicing or chopping with sharp knives.

● Turn pan handles to the side so that you can't knock them over.

● If you spill anything on the floor, mop it up right away.

● Take great care when you are frying food, or using hot water.

● Have a heatproof mat or chopping board to put hot dishes on.

● Wear oven mitts to lift things in and out of the oven.

● Never leave the kitchen when gas or electric burners are on.

● If you can, wash dirty dishes as you go, to clear space.

About measuring

Ingredients are measured in grams, litres and millilitres as well as pounds, ounces and cups in this book.

Just follow one set of measurements carefully.

Most recipes in this book are enough for four people to eat. You can multiply the ingredients for more people, or divide them for fewer.

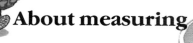

'1 tbs' means one tablespoonful. It should be flat, or level, across the top, not heaped.

'1 tsp' means one level teaspoonful.

A *'pinch'* of something means about the amount that you can pinch between your thumb and your forefinger.

Cookery tips

Here are some tips you will find useful as you cook some of the recipes in this book.

Separating an egg

Gently crack the egg on the edge of a bowl. Pull the shell apart, keeping the egg in one half. Carefully tip the yolk from one half to the other a few times so the white drops into the bowl. Slide the yolk into a cup if it's not needed right away.

Heating fat

Cooking oil, butter, margarine, shortening and lard are all types of fat. You need to take great care when heating fat as it gets very hot quickly and can pop and catch fire. Only heat it until a faint, shimmery haze rises above the pan.

Watery eyes

Onions and green onions can make your eyes water when you chop them. Try rinsing these vegetables in cold water before you start chopping them up.

Greasing pans

To keep food from sticking in a tray or pan, wipe it all over inside using a paper towel dipped in shortening or vegetable oil, and line the base with waxed paper. Place the pan on the paper and draw around it for the shape.

Cookery words

Here are some words used in cookery that you may find in this book. Check what they mean here if you are not sure when you read them in a recipe.

Cream: mix fat and sugar into a cream with a wooden spoon or electric mixer.

Rub in: mixing fat and flour by rubbing them with your fingertips.

Beat: mix together by stirring very hard with a wooden spoon or electric mixer.

Fold in: mix two things using a gentle, slicing movement with a metal spoon.

Simmer: cook over a low heat, so that the food or water bubbles gently.

Blend: make something into a smooth paste, usually in an electric blender.

Fry: cook in a little hot fat (oil, butter, lard, shortening or margarine).

Whisk: add air by beating very fast with a hand whisk. (Or use an electric one.)

Bring to a boil: cook at a high heat, until the food or water bubbles.

Knead: squeeze and stretch dough to make it ready for baking.

Sift/sieve: pass dry ingredients through a sieve to get any lumps out.

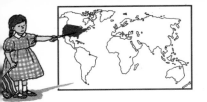

The United States

The United States, or US, is made up of 50 states. About 300 years ago, people from all over the world went to settle in this huge country. They took recipes from their homelands with them, so American cooking is made up of lots of different styles. Here are two recipes that are popular all over the US today.

Pancakes

Traditional American pancakes are quite small and thick. They are often called flapjacks. People eat them for breakfast with bacon and eggs or with sweet maple syrup. This mixture makes about ten pancakes.

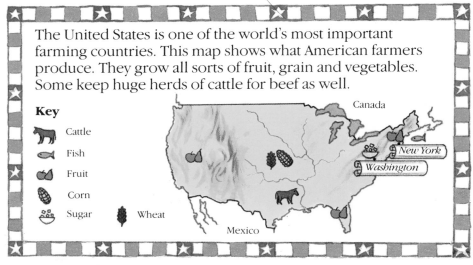

The United States is one of the world's most important farming countries. This map shows what American farmers produce. They grow all sorts of fruit, grain and vegetables. Some keep huge herds of cattle for beef as well.

Key

Cattle
Fish
Fruit
Corn
Sugar   Wheat

Canada
New York
Washington
Mexico

You will need:

150g/1 cup plain flour
2 tsp baking powder
pinch salt
1 egg

3 tbs vegetable oil
300ml/1 cup milk
maple syrup, maple-flavored syrup or warmed jam

1. Sift the flour, baking powder and salt into a medium-sized mixing bowl.

2. In another bowl, whisk the egg, 2 tbs of the oil and the milk together.

3. Beat this liquid into the flour. You may cover the bowl with cling wrap and refrigerate for half an hour.

4. Pour the last 1 tbs of oil into a frying pan. Heat it until a faint haze rises from the pan.

Make them about 10cm (4ins) wide.

5. Using a ladle, slowly pour two or three small pools of pancake mixture into the pan.

6. When the pancakes bubble, flip them over and cook the other side. Serve them right away.

Slow syrup

Maple syrup comes from the sap of maple trees. Each tree produces only about two bottles of syrup in a whole year.

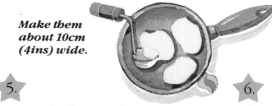

Maple syrup is quite expensive. Maple-flavored syrup is cheaper and tastes just as good.

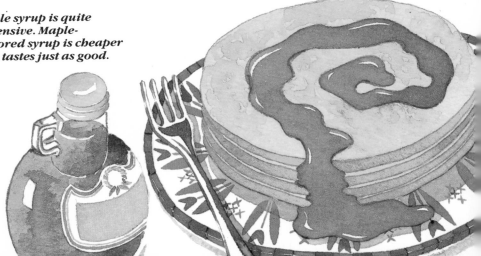

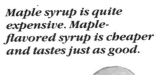

Thanksgiving

On November 28, 1621, some early American settlers cooked a turkey to thank God for their first harvest. Today, this day is a holiday called Thanksgiving. Americans still cook turkey to celebrate it.

Hamburgers

The first hamburgers were made in Hamburg, Germany. German settlers probably first took the recipe to America, but American cooks have made hamburgers famous around the world.

You will need:

1lb lean ground beef
about ½ tsp salt
about ¼ tsp pepper
4 hamburger buns, split

4 lettuce leaves
sliced dill pickles
mayonnaise
mustard
ketchup
sliced cheese

1 sliced tomato
1 sliced onion

1.

Mix ground beef, onion and as much or as little salt and pepper as you like.

2.

Shape mixture into 4 patties, ½ inch thick.

3.

Grill the insides of the buns until lightly browned. Keep warm in a very low oven.

Pastry brush

4.

To charcoal-grill, place on grill 4 to 6 inches from hot coals. Some people like to brush the patties with a little oil.

5.

Cook, turning once, 12 minutes or until done.
To panfry, cook patties in skillet over medium heat for about 7 minutes, turning frequently.

6.

To broil, set oven at broil. Cook hamburgers about 6 inches from heat approximately 4 minutes for each side.

Serve with relishes such as mustard, mayonnaise, tomato ketchup, chopped onion and dill pickles.

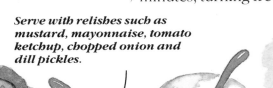

7.

Serve on toasted buns with a choice of toppings such as chili, mushrooms, bacon, green peppers or jalapeno peppers.

Banana milkshake

Milkshakes go well with hamburgers. Here's how to make a fresh banana milkshake for one.

You will need:

300ml/1 cup milk
1 chopped banana

Put the milk and the banana in a blender for about two minutes. Pour into a tall glass and serve with a straw. You could add a scoop of vanilla ice cream too.

Latin America

All the land between Mexico and the bottom of Argentina is known as Latin America. The main cooking ingredients of these countries are tomatoes, hot chili peppers and beans, often served in shells made from corn flour. Some recipes were first made by tribes of Indians who lived in Latin America centuries ago, such as the Aztecs, Mayas and Incas.

Latin America contains mountain ranges, rainforests, plains called pampas, lush valleys and steamy swamps. Farmers use the land in lots of different ways. They grow many crops and keep beef cattle.

United States

Mexico

Mexico City

Peru

Lima

Brazil

Rio de Janeiro

Key

🐄 Cattle

Cocoa

☕ Coffee

Fruit

Corn

🐑 Sheep

Tropical fruit

Wheat

Chile

Argentina

Buenos Aires

Refried beans

Latin American cooks use beans in lots of different ways. Here, cooked, canned beans are mashed and then cooked again in a frying pan.

You will need:

1 400g/14oz can kidney beans
1 medium onion

1 clove of garlic, peeled
pinch of salt
30g/2 tbs lard or margarine
60g/¼ cup grated cheese

1. Peel and chop the onion. Crush the garlic clove with a fork or in a garlic crusher.

2. Melt the fat in a frying pan until a haze rises. Fry the onions and garlic until soft.

Sprinkle on the grated cheese just before you eat.

3. Mash the drained beans into the mixture with a fork. Fry them until fully hot, then serve.

Tacos

Tacos are crisp corn shells stuffed with meat, fish, salad and tasty toppings such as guacamole and refried beans. Lots of stores now sell tacos that just need baking for two minutes before you fill them yourself.

1. Here are some ideas for cooked meat or fish to put in the bottom of tacos.

Fry 250g (½lb) of ground beef, a little chopped onion, salt and pepper for about 15 minutes.

Try mixing a can of tuna with a little lemon juice and salt and pepper. Add some mayonnaise if you like.

You could chop two cooked chicken breasts into very small pieces. Add salt and pepper and lemon juice.

Guacamole

Guacamole is a creamy mixture made from avocados. The Aztecs probably made it first, 500 years ago. You can eat it on its own as a spicy dip, or as a filling in tacos (see below).

(see below)

You will need:

2 soft, ripe avocados
1 small can tomatoes
½ a small onion, chopped

2 tbs olive oil
pinch salt and pepper
1 tbs lemon juice
pinch chili powder

Use an electric blender if you can.

1.
Seed

Cut the avocados in half lengthwise around the seed. Pull the halves apart and take out the seed. Scoop the flesh into a bowl.

2.
Add all the other ingredients to the avocado. Mix in a blender, or with a fork or potato masher, until the mixture is smooth.

3.
Pour your guacamole into a bowl. Serve it as soon as you can, as it turns brown if you leave it for too long.

These tortilla chips, made from corn flour, are delicious dipped in guacamole. Many stores sell them.

Salsas

In Latin America, people serve hot, spicy sauces, called salsas, with many meals. Some salsas are made with so much fresh chilli that they can actually burn your mouth.

Tomato salsa

You will need:

2 tomatoes, peeled (see page 14)
1 small onion
1 tsp chili powder
pinch salt and pepper
2 chopped parsley sprigs
pinch sugar

(see page 14)

Chop the tomatoes and onions. Mix all the ingredients together and serve in a bowl. Add more chili powder if you like really hot flavors.

Tomato salsa is crunchy and mild.

A variety of salsas may be on the table at once, for people to choose from.

2.
Cut strips of lettuce and slices of tomato. Put them on top of the meat or fish.

3.
Spoon some refried beans and guacamole into each taco. Top with grated cheese.

The Caribbean

The Caribbean is made up of more than 20 islands. Over the centuries, many different peoples have lived on them. Each one planted their own crops and cooked them in different ways. Today, Caribbean food is an exciting mixture of several cooking styles. It is often known as Creole cooking. These two recipes use two of the many exotic Caribbean fruits.

Mango ice cream

Mangoes are delicately flavored fruit that grow in the Caribbean. Many supermarkets sell fresh mangoes. Delicatessens and health food stores sell them in cans. Here they are made into ice cream.

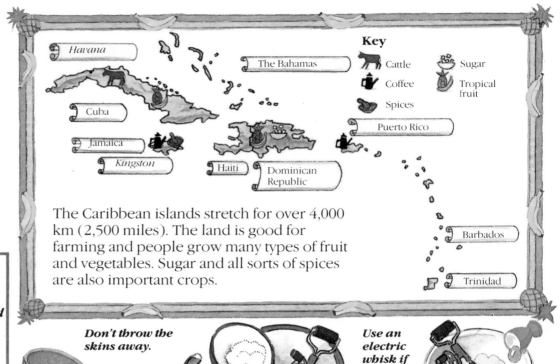

Key

🐄 Cattle
☕ Coffee
🦐 Spices
🍬 Sugar
🍍 Tropical fruit

Havana · *The Bahamas* · *Cuba* · *Jamaica* · *Kingston* · *Haiti* · *Dominican Republic* · *Puerto Rico* · *Barbados* · *Trinidad*

The Caribbean islands stretch for over 4,000 km (2,500 miles). The land is good for farming and people grow many types of fruit and vegetables. Sugar and all sorts of spices are also important crops.

You will need:

4 eggs, separated (see page 5)
120g/½ cup granulated sugar
300ml/1 cup heavy cream
2 mangoes or 2 medium cans of mango pulp
1 tsp lemon juice

❄ *Turn the control knob on your freezer to 'maximum' before you start. Turn it up after step 6.*

Don't throw the skins away.

1. Empty the canned pulp into a bowl, or cut both fresh mangoes in half and dig out their flat seeds. Scoop the flesh into a bowl.

Use an electric whisk if you can.

2. Whisk the egg whites until you can pull blobs up with your whisk to stand up in points. Add the sugar and whisk for two more minutes.

3. In another bowl, whisk the cream until it is very thick. Add the egg yolks one by one, whisking the mixture a little after each one.

4. Making small, gentle cutting movements with a metal spoon, add the cream mixture to the egg whites. Don't stir too hard.

Set an alarm clock to go off in 1½ hours to remind you.

5. Add the mashed mango and lemon juice in the same way as step 4. Pour it all into a tub with a lid. Freeze with the lid on for 1½ hours.

6. Scoop the mixture into a bowl and whisk it for two minutes. Pour it back into the tub and freeze until it is solid, as ice cream should be.

Don't forget to turn your freezer up when the ice cream is ready.

Try serving your ice cream in the hollowed-out mango skins.

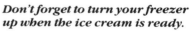

Banana bread

Bananas are an important food in the Caribbean. People cook and eat them in many different ways. You can eat this banana bread buttered, or with some cream, as a dessert.

You will need:

120g/½ cup butter or margarine
90g/⅓ cup granulated sugar
90g/⅓ cup brown sugar, firmly packed
1 egg
250g/1½ cups whole wheat flour
2 tsp baking powder
pinch salt
pinch nutmeg
1 tsp vanilla
2 large bananas
90g/⅔ cup raisins
90g/¾ cup chopped walnuts
2 tbs milk

 Set the oven to 180°C(350°F)/ Gas mark 4

Fantasy islands

When the explorer Christopher Columbus first saw the islands of the Caribbean, he thought he had reached Paradise because they were so beautiful.

This is hard work at first.

1. Cut the butter into cubes. Using a wooden spoon, cream the butter and all the sugar together until smooth.

If the mixture gets lumpy, stir in a spoonful of the flour mixture

3. In a cup, beat the egg and the milk together with a fork. Beat them into the butter mixture gradually.

5. Peel the bananas and mash them with a fork. Add the vanilla to them, and stir them into the main mixture.

7. Bake the banana bread for about one hour, or until a skewer or toothpick comes out clean when you stick it into the loaf.

2. Sift the flour, baking powder, nutmeg and salt into another bowl. Add the raisins and nuts and stir well.

4. Make slicing movements with a metal spoon to mix the flour mixture gently into the butter and egg mixture.

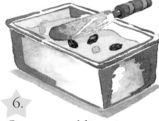

6. Grease and line (see page 5) a loaf pan. Pour the mixture in and smooth the top with a knife.

8. Run a blunt knife between the loaf and the pan. Put a wire rack on the pan and turn both over. Tap to make the loaf drop.

Exotic fruits

Some of the most exotic fruit and vegetables in the world grow on the islands of the Caribbean. Today, you can see many of them in our supermarkets. Here are some to try.

This fruit is a papaya or pawpaw. It is delicious with lemon juice.

Caribbean cooks use a lot of sweet, white coconut flesh and its see-through milk.

This fruit is called an ackee. People say it tastes like scrambled egg.

Caribbean farmers grow a lot of pineapples. They send them all around the world.

Put your bread in a covered container when it is cool, to keep it fresh.

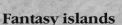

11

Africa

Africa is made up of more than 40 separate countries. Each one has its own traditional dishes, but cooking styles are similar. African cooks have to use whatever crops grow nearby, so they cook different sorts of food in different parts of this huge continent.

There are deserts, mountains, swamps, plains and jungles in Africa. Farmers grow whatever they can in each area. In some places, so little rain falls that it is difficult to grow enough food for everybody.

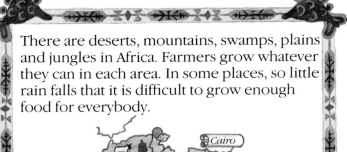

Key

Cattle		Peanuts	
Citrus fruit		Sheep	
Cocoa		Sugar	
Corn		Tropical fruit	
		Wheat	

Peanut bread

Peanuts, or groundnuts, are an important crop in many parts of Africa. Here, they are made into a sort of bread. It will keep for days in a covered pan.

You will need:

60g/½ cup unsalted shelled peanuts
375g/2½ cups plain flour
3 tsp baking powder
30g/¼ cup granulated sugar
pinch salt
1 egg
300ml/1 cup milk

Set the oven to 180°C(350°F)/ Gas mark 4

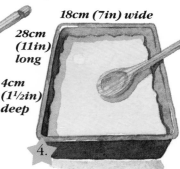

1. Chop the peanuts in a blender or put them in a plastic bag and roll a rolling pin over them.

2. Sift the flour, salt and baking powder into a mixing bowl. Using a fork, beat the egg in a cup.

3. Stir the beaten egg, sugar, milk and peanuts into the flour. Spoon into a greased pan.

18cm (7in) wide
28cm (11in) long
4cm (1½in) deep

4. Smooth the top and leave for 20 minutes. This makes the cooked bread a lighter and more even texture.

5. Bake the bread for half an hour until golden. When cool, cut squares to eat with cheese or jam.

Bobotie

This is a traditional dish in South Africa. People from all over the world have settled there. The food they make today shows this, as it mixes so many different flavors.

You will need:

500g/1lb ground beef
2 slices bread
30g/2 tbs butter
300ml/1 cup milk
1 onion, chopped
1 garlic clove, crushed
60g/⅓ cup dried apricots, chopped

60g/½ cup flaked almonds
60g/½ cup raisins
½ tsp chili powder
1 tsp curry powder
2 tbs lemon juice
2 eggs
pinch salt and pepper

 Set the oven to 170°C(325°F)/ Gas mark 3

1. Rip the bread into pieces. Put it in a shallow dish and pour half the milk over it. Let it soak.

2. Melt the butter in a frying pan. Fry the meat, onions and garlic for about five minutes, stirring all the time.

3. In a bowl, mix the curry and chili powders, lemon juice, salt and pepper. Stir in the meat gradually.

4. Add the nuts, raisins, apricots and soaked bread. Stir in any milk that is left in the dish the bread soaked in.

5. Press the hot mixture into an ovenproof dish. Whisk the two eggs and the rest of the milk. Pour them over the top.

6. Bake your bobotie for one hour. The egg and milk will set like a golden custard. Serve it right away.

Spices, such as chili and curry powder, were first used in Africa to hide the taste of meat that had spoiled in the hot climate.

African vegetables

In Africa, cooks make vegetables into dumplings or pastes called fufus. They make a meal more filling, as rice, potatoes or bread do in other countries.

This is a cassava root. It can be dried, ground and made into dumplings.

Plantains are a large, green sort of banana. They can be made into dumplings, too.

Yams are peeled and softened in hot water. People make them into fried yam balls.

Corn is made into corn flour. When mixed with water, it makes a mashed paste called ugali.

13

Spain and Portugal

The traditional dishes of these two countries tell a fascinating story. Around 500 years ago, Spanish and Portuguese sailors conquered South America and lands in the East. They brought back food that people at home had never seen before, such as tomatoes, peppers and new spices. Cooks in Spain and Portugal mixed these ingredients with ones that grew at home in recipes such as these.

Gazpacho

This tangy Spanish soup is called gazpacho. It is very refreshing as it is served ice cold. It was probably first made out of leftover salad.

You will need:

6 green onions
6 ripe tomatoes
½ a cucumber
1 clove of garlic, peeled

1 green pepper
1 slice of bread
2 tbs olive oil
2 tbs wine vinegar
or lemon juice

pinch salt and
pepper
120ml/½ cup very
cold water

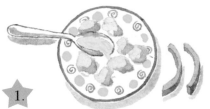

The skins should peel off easily.

1. Cut the crusts off the bread. Crumble the bread into a saucer. Add the vinegar or lemon juice. Let it soak.

2. To skin the tomatoes, lower them into a bowl of boiling water for two minutes, then into one of cold water for two minutes.

3. Chop the onion, pepper, cucumber and peeled tomatoes. Crush the peeled garlic clove in a crusher or with a fork.

4. Put the vegetables and soaked bread in a blender for three minutes, or push them very hard through a sieve with a spoon.

5. When the mixture is smooth, add 120ml (½ cup) cold water. Pour your soup into a serving bowl. Stir in the olive oil.

Sardine salad

Portuguese cooks use a lot of fish. Here, sardines are made into an appetizer.

You will need:

4 lemons
2 cans sardines
2 tbs vinegar

2 tomatoes,
chopped
4 black olives
salt, pepper

1. Cut the top third off each lemon. Scoop the flesh into a bowl. Mix the sardines, salt, pepper and vinegar with it.

2. Spoon 1 tbs chopped tomato into each lemon case. Fill them up with the sardine mixture and put a black olive on top.

In Spain, gazpacho is often served with bowls of chopped fresh vegetables, like these.

6. Sprinkle with salt and pepper. Cover the bowl with cling wrap and put in the refrigerator for an hour before serving.

Paella

This dish, called paella, is a whole meal in itself. Spanish cooks believe that food should look as good as it tastes, so try to make your paella really bright and colorful.

You will need:

1 medium onion
1 red pepper
1 small can tomatoes
1 clove of garlic
2 skinned chicken breasts
bouillon cube
450ml/1½ cups boiling water

250g/3 cups long grain rice
120g/4oz shrimps, cooked and cleaned
60g/½ cup frozen peas
2 tbs vegetable oil
1 tsp saffron or turmeric
pinch salt and pepper

To decorate:

6 fresh mussels
1 lemon
sprig of fresh parsley

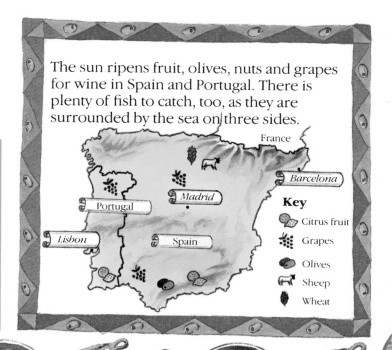

The sun ripens fruit, olives, nuts and grapes for wine in Spain and Portugal. There is plenty of fish to catch, too, as they are surrounded by the sea on three sides.

France
Barcelona
Madrid
Portugal
Lisbon
Spain

Key
Citrus fruit
Grapes
Olives
Sheep
Wheat

1.

Chop the onions, red pepper, and tomatoes into small pieces. Peel and crush the garlic clove with a fork or crusher.

2.

Slice the chicken. Heat the oil in a large frying pan that has a lid. Fry the chicken until it turns white on the outside.

3.

Add the onion, garlic, salt and pepper. Fry them until they are quite soft. Add the tomatoes and red pepper to the pan and stir well.

4.

Pour the boiling water onto the bouillon cube in a measuring cup. Stir it until dissolved. Carefully pour the broth into the pan.

5.

If the rice sticks, add a little more water.

Add the rice and stir in the saffron or turmeric. Put the lid on the pan and cook over a low heat for about 15 minutes.

6.

If any mussels don't open, they are bad. Throw them away.

Stir in the shrimps and peas. Arrange the mussels on top and cook your paella for five more minutes with the lid on.

7.

Cut a lemon into wedges. Arrange them on top of the paella. Sprinkle with some parsley and serve hot.

Favorite fish

Dried cod is a Portuguese speciality. Each fish is sprinkled with salt and dried for several months before it is cooked.

Paella is often cooked and served in a pan like this. It is called a paellera.

France

France is famous for food and cooking. The French for a cook is 'chef de cuisine', which means 'head of the kitchen'. Many important cooking techniques came from French chefs.

In France, lots of people enjoy spending a long time cooking and eating meals. These two French dishes will not take too long to make, but look good and taste delicious.

Salade niçoise

This colorful fish salad was first made in the city of Nice, in the south of France. It is called 'salade niçoise', which means 'salad from Nice'.

You will need:

2 eggs
4 tomatoes
1 lettuce
1 green pepper
1 can anchovies

1 small can French-style beans
1 medium can of tuna, drained
a few black olives
sprig of fresh parsley

The yolks will turn gray if you don't do this.

1.

Boil the eggs for ten minutes. Then plunge them into cold water. When cool, tap and peel off their shells.

2.

Wash the lettuce and gently dry it with paper towels. Arrange the leaves in the bottom of a big salad bowl.

3.

Sprinkle on the beans. Dice the pepper and cut three tomatoes into quarters. Arrange them around the bowl.

4.

Make a mound of tuna in the middle of the salad. Pour the oil off the anchovies and lay them over the top.

5.

Decorate with slices of hard-boiled egg and olives. Top with slices of the fourth tomato and parsley.

French dressing

Some people add a sauce to salad, called a dressing. The simplest dressing is called 'vinaigrette', or French dressing. It was first made in France.

You will need:

4 tbs olive oil
4 tsp vinegar
1 tsp mustard
(Dijon is best)
pinch granulated sugar
pinch salt and pepper

Pour all the ingredients into a jar with a screw-on top. Put the top on and shake hard. Pour the mixture over the salad just before serving.

Truffle-hunters

In France, pigs and dogs are trained to sniff out especially tasty mushrooms, called truffles. They grow under the ground. Good ones are very expensive.

French apple tart

France is famous for its pastries and cakes. Shops called 'patisseries' sell them. This tart recipe comes from northern France, where farmers grow a lot of apples.

You will need:

180g/1¼ cups plain flour
90g/5 tbs butter or margarine, cut into cubes
60g/¼ cup granulated sugar
1 egg
3 green apples
3 red apples
2 tbs apricot jam

Set the oven to 200°C(400°F)/ Gas mark 6

1. Peel the green apples and cut them into quarters. Cut out the cores and slice the quarters up thinly.

2. Put the apples in a pan with 2 tbs water. Cook them over a low heat until soft (about five minutes). Stir with a wooden spoon.

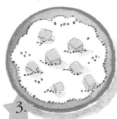

Keep rubbing until the mixture looks like crumbs.

3. Sift the flour into a bowl. Add the butter cubes and rub them between your fingertips in the bowl of flour.

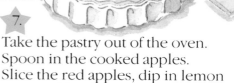

Add a couple of drops of water if it is too dry to stick together.

4. Separate the egg (see page 5). Add the sugar and the egg yolk to the flour mixture and squeeze it gently into a ball.

Push the rolling pin away from you. Turn the board if you need to.

5. Sprinkle some flour onto a board and a rolling pin. Roll the pastry until it is about 26cm (10in) wide and 2cm (⅛in) thick.

If the pastry breaks, press it in a piece at a time.

6. Line a 20cm (9in) pie plate with pastry. Trim the edges and put in the refrigerator for 30 minutes. Then bake for five minutes.

With a fork, prick the crust all over.

Make the slices overlap, like this.

7. Take the pastry out of the oven. Spoon in the cooked apples. Slice the red apples, dip in lemon juice and lay them in circles on top.

8. Mix the jam with 2 tbs hot water and spread it over the apples. Bake your tart for about 30 mins, until golden on top.

France is the biggest farming country in Europe. It sends food such as cheese, fruit and vegetables all over the world. French grapes are used to make wine, too.

Key

- Cattle
- Fish
- Fruit
- Grapes
- Pigs
- Sheep
- Vegetables
- Wheat

British Isles
Belgium
Germany
Paris
Switzerland
Bordeaux
Italy
Nice
Spain

The British Isles

There are five countries in the British Isles. They are England, Scotland, Ireland, Northern Ireland and Wales. Each country has its own traditional dishes, but cooking styles are similar everywhere. Here are two well-known British recipes for you to try.

 Irish Stew

Stew is a mixture of meat and vegetables. It is cooked for a very long time to make the meat tender and blend all the flavors together. This tasty stew recipe is from Ireland.

You will need:

750g/1½lbs lamb (cubed stewing lamb or neck or shoulder joints)
750g/1½lbs potatoes
2 large onions

1 tsp mixed herbs
1 beef bouillon cube
450ml/1½ cups boiling water
pinch salt and pepper

 Set the oven to 170°C(325°F)/ Gas mark 3

1.
If you are using a lamb joint, cut it into cubes 2cm (1in) big, on a chopping board. This is tricky, so ask for help.

2.
Peel the potatoes and cut them into slices about 1cm (½in) thick. Peel and chop the onions into small pieces.

Use a dish with a lid.

3.
Cover the bottom of a large dish with meat cubes. Add a layer of onions, then put a layer of potato slices on top.

Make the top layer potato slices.

4.
Continue adding layers of meat, onions and then potatoes until the dish is full. Sprinkle with the herbs, salt and pepper.

5.
In a cup, dissolve the bouillon cube in the boiling water. Slowly pour the broth liquid into the dish and put the lid on.

6.
Put the dish on a baking sheet to catch spills. Cook the stew for about two hours. After one hour, add some water if it looks dry.

Sunday lunch

Traditionally, lunch on Sunday is roast meat and vegetables in the British Isles.

With roast lamb, people serve a sauce made from mint leaves and vinegar. Apple sauce comes with roast pork. With roast beef, cooks make a mixture of eggs, milk and flour called Yorkshire pudding.

In Ireland, a dish called Colcannon is often served with Irish Stew. It is made of mashed potatoes and boiled cabbage.

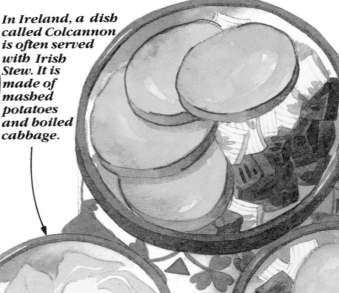

Scones

Scones are small cakes. People often split them in half and spread them with butter, jam or cream. This recipe makes about 12 scones.

You will need:

250g/1½ cups self-rising flour
60g/¼ cup butter, cut into cubes
60g/¼ cup granulated sugar

4 tbs milk
pinch salt

 Set the oven to
220°C(425°F)
Gas mark 7

Farming land is limited in the British Isles. Fruit, vegetables and grain grow on the best land. Sheep and cows graze in fields and on moors and hills.

Scotland

Edinburgh

N. Ireland

Belfast

Dublin

England

Wales

Ireland

Cardiff

London

Key

Deer

Cattle

Sheep

Fish

Sugar

Wheat

Potatoes

Fruit

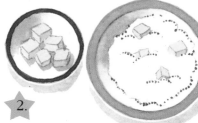

1.
Sift the flour into a mixing bowl to get rid of any lumps. Add the pinch of salt.

2.
Rub the butter cubes into the flour with your fingertips until the mixture is like breadcrumbs.

Add 1 tsp of water if it is too dry to stick together.

3.
Add the sugar and milk and gently squeeze the mixture into a ball with your fingers.

4.
Roll the mixture out on a floured board or counter until it is about 1.5cm (¾in) thick.

5.
Cut circles out of the mixture with a round cutter or a cup. Put them onto a greased cookie sheet.

6.
Bake your scones for about ten minutes, until brown on top. Let them cool on a rack.

Tasty seaweed

In South Wales, people cook a seaweed called laver that they collect on the beach. They mix it with oatmeal and fry it. Then, it is called laverbread.

This kind of thick cream is called clotted cream.

Cut your scones in half like this.

Tea in the British Isles is often a meal of scones with other cakes and cups of tea, served in the late afternoon.

Italy

Italy has been famous for its cooking since the Ancient Romans ruled there, over 2,000 years ago. Today, people all over the world eat some traditional Italian dishes, such as spaghetti bolognese and pizza. In Italy, cooks take great care choosing and cooking their ingredients.

Pizza Margherita

Pizzas were first made in the southern Italian city of Naples. They can have many different toppings. This one was named after the first Italian queen, Margherita. It takes about 1½ hours to make, so start cooking well before you want to eat.

> **You will need:**
> *250g/1½ cups bread flour*
> *1 tbs/½ oz dried yeast*
> *or use 'easy-blend' yeast, as the packet says*
> *1 tbs sugar*
> *150ml/½ cup warm water*
> *400g/14oz can tomatoes*
> *2 tbs tomato paste*
> *60g/1 cup grated mozarella cheese*
> *½ tsp dried oregano*
> *pinch salt and black pepper*

You can serve pizza hot or cold.

1. Mix the sugar and dried yeast with 2 tbs of the warm water in a small bowl. Leave in a warm place for 10-15 minutes or until it turns light and frothy on top.

Pull the mixture in from the sides of the bowl with your fingers.

2. Sift the flour and salt into another bowl. Make a hollow in the middle and pour in the yeast and the rest of the warm water. Gently squeeze into a ball.

A crisp salad goes well with slices of pizza.

This is called kneading.

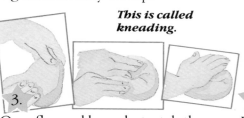

3. On a floured board, stretch the dough out, then fold it over. Press down on it with your palm, turn the dough around and do the same movements again.

The dough will grow to double its size.

4. When the dough is soft and stretchy, put it in a bowl covered with a cloth in a warm place for an hour. After 45 minutes, set the oven to 230°C(450°F)/Gas mark 8.

Try putting other toppings, such as fried onions, grilled bacon bits, olives, peppers, mushrooms, sweetcorn, pineapple, or tuna onto your pizza base.

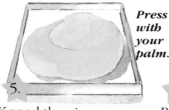

Press with your palm.

5. Knead the risen dough a little more. On a greased cookie sheet, press it into a round shape about 1cm (½in) thick and 30cm (12in) wide.

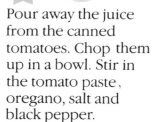

6. Pour away the juice from the canned tomatoes. Chop them up in a bowl. Stir in the tomato paste, oregano, salt and black pepper.

7. Spread the tomato mixture evenly over the pizza base. Sprinkle with the grated cheese and cook for about 25 minutes, until golden on top.

In the colder region of northern Italy, farmers grow wheat and keep cows for milk and cheese. Farther south, fruit, grapes for wine, and vegetables ripen in the hot summer sun.

Switzerland

Austria

Parma

Venice

Bologna

Key

Cattle

Citrus fruit

Rome

Fish

Naples

Grapes

Olives

Sugar

Sicily

Spaghetti Bolognese

Bolognese sauce was first made in the city of Bologna, in northern Italy. It is traditionally served on top of spaghetti.

You will need:

500g/1lb ground beef
3 strips of bacon, cut into pieces 2cm (1in) wide
1 medium onion, chopped
1 medium carrot, chopped
60g/3/4 cup mushrooms, sliced
1 clove of garlic, peeled and crushed
1 16oz can tomatoes
2 tbs tomato paste
90g/6 tbs butter
1/2 tsp dried oregano
1/2 tsp dried basil
salt and black pepper
375g/12oz spaghetti

Pasta

Spaghetti is one of over 50 sorts of Italian pasta. Pasta means 'dough' or 'paste' in Italian. It is made of flour, eggs and salt mixed together. It should be cooked 'al dente', which means soft but not soggy.

Pasta sheets are called lasagne. Cooks put meat between layers of lasagne, with sauce on top.

These pasta tubes are called macaroni. They are often served in cheese sauce.

Pasta can be made into fancy shapes, like these.

This pasta has some whole wheat flour in it.

If spinach is added to pasta, it is called 'pasta verde', which means 'green pasta' in Italian.

These pasta envelopes are called ravioli. They are stuffed with meat.

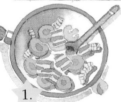

1.

Make sure you use a pan that has a lid.

Melt half the butter. Fry the bacon, garlic, onion, carrot and mushrooms in it for three minutes.

2.

Add the beef and cook it until it browns. Add the tomato paste, canned tomatoes, basil and oregano.

3.

Add 4 tbs water and simmer the sauce for 20 minutes, with the lid on. Stir it quickly after ten minutes.

Eating spaghetti

Eating spaghetti is tricky. Try winding it around a fork. Use a spoon to keep it from slipping off the bottom.

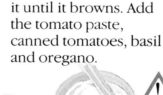

⚠

4.

Boil 750ml (3 cups) of water in a pan. Put the spaghetti ends in, then slowly push it all in as it softens.

Make a sauce with tomatoes and vegetables if you are vegetarian.

5.

Boil the spaghetti for about eight minutes. Then pour it into a colander over the sink to drain it.

6.

Lift the spaghetti onto four plates, using two forks. It's slippery, so doing it quickly is best.
Add the rest of the butter and spoon on some bolognese sauce.

Italians sprinkle grated cheese from the town of Parma onto spaghetti. It is called Parmesan.

The Netherlands

The Netherlands is also called Holland, and people from here are known as Dutch. Food in the Netherlands is simple and wholesome. It is a very flat country, so icy cold winds blow right across it in winter. Many traditional Dutch recipes were first made to warm people up on cold days.

Cauliflower in cheese sauce

Holland is famous for its cheeses. Here, cheese is made into a hot, creamy sauce to pour over vegetables. Use a Dutch cheese, such as Gouda or Edam, if you can.

You will need:

1 large cauliflower   *300ml/1 cup milk*
30g/2 tbs butter   *120g/½ cup grated cheese*
30g/2 tbs flour   *pinch salt and pepper*

1.

Remove the cauliflower leaves and cut it into four pieces. Cook in boiling water for ten minutes, then drain at once.

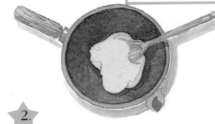

2.

Melt the butter in a pan. With a wooden spoon, stir in the flour, salt and pepper to make a smooth paste. Cook for one minute.

3.

Remove pan from the heat, gradually stir in the milk. Put back on the heat, bring the sauce to a boil, stirring all the time.

4.

Then turn the heat off. Stir in most of the grated cheese. Drain the cauliflower and pour it into a heat-proof dish. Pour the cheese sauce over it.

5.

Sprinkle on the rest of the cheese. Put the whole dish under the broiler until the top starts to bubble and turns brown.

Try serving thick slices of brown bread and butter with this dish.

Cheese races

Some Dutch towns hold weekly cheese markets. It is a tradition for cheese carriers to race each other to see who can carry their load the fastest.

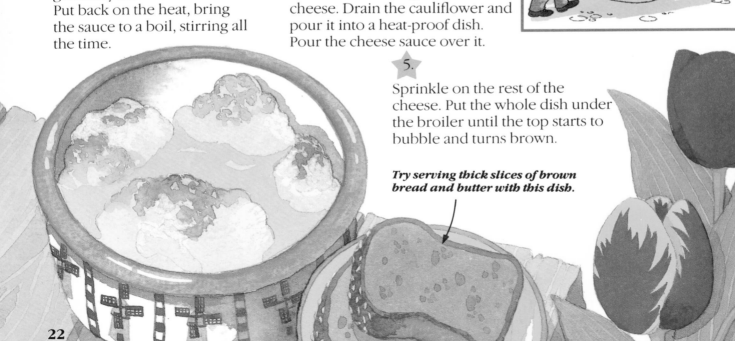

Fruit tarts

This recipe for fruit tarts comes from the city of Limburg, in the southern Netherlands. The tarts have a bread base, so they take some time to make, but they are delicious.

You will need:

250g/1½ cups bread flour
1 tbs/½ oz dried yeast or use 'easy-blend' yeast, as the packet says
60g/¼ cup sugar

1 egg
6 tsp warm milk
30g/2 tbs butter
180g/1 cup fresh or canned cherries or plums. (For sweeter taste, use canned pie filling.)

Spicy banquet

Rijsttafel, (which means rice table in Dutch), is a banquet of up to 25 different dishes served with rice. Dutch traders brought the recipes back from the islands of Indonesia when they were there in the 1700s.

Set the oven to 200°C(400°F)/Gas mark 6

1.
Mix the dried yeast with the milk and 1 tbs of the sugar in a small bowl. Leave in a warm place until the yeast gets frothy.

2.
Melt the butter in a pan. Take it off the heat. While it cools in the pan, sift the flour, the rest of the sugar and salt into a large mixing bowl.

3.
Pour the warm butter and yeast into the flour. Beat and add the egg. Gently squeeze into a ball. Knead the dough (see step 3, page 20).

4.
Cover the bowl and leave it in a warm place for an hour. Then divide the risen dough into 4 balls, roll out to ¼ in thickness.

Sprinkle with a little more sugar if you like.

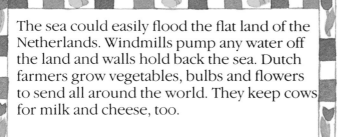

The sea could easily flood the flat land of the Netherlands. Windmills pump any water off the land and walls hold back the sea. Dutch farmers grow vegetables, bulbs and flowers to send all around the world. They keep cows for milk and cheese, too.

5.
Put the dough onto a cookie sheet. Cut open the fresh or canned fruit and take out any seeds. Arrange the fruit on the dough.

6.
Cook your tarts for 20 minutes, then turn the oven down to 180°C (350°F)/Gas mark 4 for ten more minutes. Eat them hot or cold.

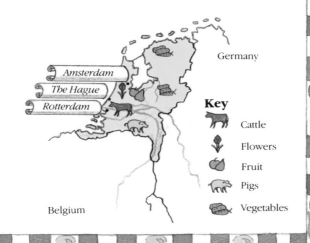

Germany

Amsterdam
The Hague
Rotterdam

Key

Cattle
Flowers
Fruit
Pigs
Vegetables

Belgium

Germany

Germany is well-known for certain sorts of food and drink. You can buy German sausages, such as frankfurters, in many countries today. Germany is also famous for its beer and white wine.

Cakes and cookies are another speciality. Typical German dishes are quite simply flavored, but very tasty. Here are two recipes that give you an idea of their style of cooking.

'Heaven and Earth'

This dish is often called 'Heaven and Earth' because it is made of apples, (which grow up in the sky) and potatoes, (which grow in the earth). It is popular as a hot lunch or supper.

You will need:

750g/1½lbs potatoes
750g/1½lbs cooking apples, peeled and cored

2 medium onions
8 frankfurters
2 tbs granulated sugar
30g/2 tbs butter
pinch salt and pepper

Along the River Rhine, farmers grow grapes for wine. In the middle of Germany, the land is used for growing grain and vegetables and for keeping pigs to make pork sausages.

Key

- Cattle
- Grapes
- Pigs
- Potatoes
- Vegetables
- Wheat

1. Peel and slice the potatoes. Put them in a pan that has a lid. Cover with water and add a pinch of salt. Boil them with the lid on for 15-20 minutes, until soft.

2. Slice the apples and put them in another pan. Add 2 tbs water and cook the apples over a low heat until they are soft (about five minutes). Then add the sugar.

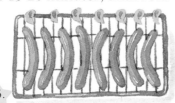 

Use a spoon to press them over to one side.

3. Cook the frankfurters. They can usually be grilled, fried or put in hot water for five minutes.

4. Peel and slice the onions. Melt the butter in a frying pan and fry the onions until they are soft and slightly brown around the edges.

5. Pour the water from the potatoes and mash them with pepper. Spoon them into one half of a casserole (a deep, oven- proof dish).

Frankfurters were first made only in the German city of Frankfurt.

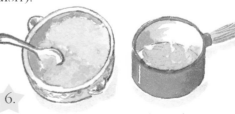

6. Spoon the apples into the other half of the dish. Arrange the cooked frankfurters on top, spoon on the fried onions and serve right away.

In Germany, they celebrate the Feast of Saint Nicholas on December 6. Children are given lots of cakes, cookies, fruit and candies. Sometimes, they get a small house made of gingerbread, like this.

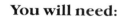

Lebkuchen

These spicy cookies are often called Lebkuchen. This means 'love cookies' in German. In south Germany, it is a tradition for lovers to give each other heart-shaped Lebkuchen. People also decorate them and hang them on Christmas trees. This mixture makes about 15 cookies.

You will need:

4 tbs clear honey
60g/¼ cup butter or margarine
250g/1½ cups plain flour
1 tsp baking powder
60g/⅓ cup brown sugar
30g/¼ cup cocoa
2 tsp dried ginger
1 tsp allspice
1 egg
90g/½ cup powdered sugar
1 tbs lemon juice

Set the oven to 200°C (400°F)/ Gas mark 6

1.

Put the honey, sugar and butter in a pan over a low heat, until the butter melts. Take the pan off the heat and let it cool.

See page 5 for how to separate an egg.

2.

Sift the flour, baking powder, cocoa, ginger and allspice into a bowl. Add the egg yolk. Set the egg white aside.

Add a few drops of water if it won't stick together.

3.

Use a metal spoon to mix the warm honey, butter and sugar into the flour. With clean hands, squeeze the mixture into a ball.

4.

Roll the mixture out on a floured board until it is ½cm (¼in) thick. Cut some shapes out with cookie cutters or a knife.

5.

Make a hole at the top of each cookie with a skewer. Lift them onto a greased cookie sheet and bake them for about ten minutes.

Shallow, oblong, metal tray.

6.

Let the cookies cool on a wire rack. Sift the powdered sugar into a bowl. Mix in 2 tsp of egg white and lemon juice to make icing.

7.

Add food coloring if you want, then spoon some icing into an icing bag. Slowly squeeze the bag over each cookie, making any pattern you like with the icing.

You can use a cone of waxed paper, with a small hole cut in one corner, instead of an icing bag.

8.

When the icing decoration is dry, you can thread ribbons through the holes in the top of your Lebkuchen and hang them up, or eat them right away.

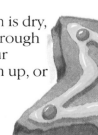

25

Central Europe

The countries between Germany in the west and Russia in the east are often called Central Europe. Winters here are very cold, so thick soups and stews fill people up and keep them warm. Rich, creamy cakes are a speciality, too.

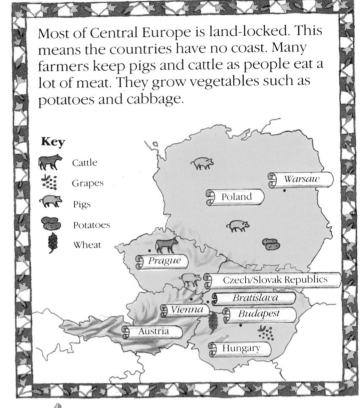

Most of Central Europe is land-locked. This means the countries have no coast. Many farmers keep pigs and cattle as people eat a lot of meat. They grow vegetables such as potatoes and cabbage.

Key

- Cattle
- Grapes
- Pigs
- Potatoes
- Wheat

Warsaw
Poland
Prague
Czech/Slovak Republics
Bratislava
Vienna
Budapest
Austria
Hungary

Hungarian goulash

Goulash is named after the Hungarian word 'gulyas', which means shepherd. Shepherds are supposed to have invented this dish. It has hot paprika in it, which is made from red peppers.

You will need:

500g/1lb stewing beef, cut into cubes
1 large onion, chopped
4 large potatoes, chopped
1 tbs cooking oil
2 tbs paprika
1 16oz can tomatoes

1 clove garlic, peeled and crushed
1 bouillon cube
450ml/1½ cups boiling water
pinch salt and black pepper
small carton sour cream or plain yogurt

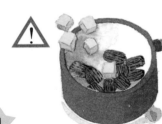

1.

Heat the oil in a large pan that has a lid. When a faint haze rises from it, fry the beef cubes until they are brown. Stir in the chopped potatoes.

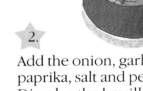

2.

Add the onion, garlic, tomatoes, paprika, salt and pepper to fry. Dissolve the bouillon cube in the boiling water and pour it in. Stir everything well.

3.

Cook your goulash with the lid on for about an hour, over a low heat. Serve it hot with a dollop of sour cream or plain yogurt on top and some rice or bread.

Dumplings

Central European cooks often add small dumplings made of dough to stews. They make the dish more filling.

You will need:

90g/²⁄₃ cup self-rising flour
1 egg
pinch salt

Mix all the ingredients together. Drop small balls of dough into your goulash ten minutes before serving.

Hungarians often eat rye bread, like this, with goulash.

Sachertorte

This rich chocolate cake was first made in 1832, by the cook Franz Sacher. He baked it for an Austrian prince. Its name means 'Sacher's cake' in German.

You will need:

150g/²⁄₃ cup margarine
150g/³⁄₄ cup granulated sugar
250g/8 oz unsweetened chocolate
6 eggs, separated
120g/³⁄₄ cup plain flour sifted
150g/¹⁄₂ cup apricot jam
2 tbs butter
250g/2 cups powdered sugar
30g/¹⁄₄ cup cocoa

Set the oven to 170°C(325°F) Gas mark 3

1.

Mix the margarine and sugar together with a wooden spoon until they are soft and creamy. Beat in the egg yolks one by one.

Wear an oven mitt to lift the hot bowl.

2.

Put half the chocolate into a small pan and place in a larger pan of boiling water. Stir until smooth, then add it to the mixture.

Always use a clean whisk.

3.

In another bowl, whisk the egg whites until they form stiff peaks.

4.

With a metal spoon, fold in the sifted flour one spoonful at a time. Then fold in the egg whites in the same way.

5.

Pour into two greased and lined cake pans, 20cm (8in) wide. Bake for 35 minutes, or until a toothpick inserted comes out clean.

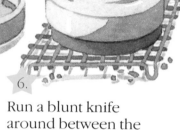

6.

Run a blunt knife around between the pan and the cake. Turn the pan over onto a wire rack and tap it to make the cake drop out.

See-through strudels

The best-known Austrian cakes are apple strudels. Cooks make the strudel pastry so thin that you can read a newspaper through a single sheet of it, people say.

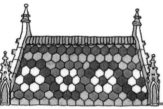

7.

Melt the rest of the chocolate (see step 2). Mix into a paste with the butter and 1 tbs of the powdered sugar. Spread it over one cake half.

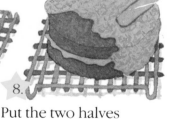

8.

Put the two halves together. Stir the jam well, then spread it in a thin layer all over the top and sides of the cake with a knife.

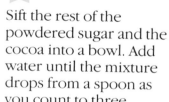

Don't make the icing too runny.

9.

Sift the rest of the powdered sugar and the cocoa into a bowl. Add water until the mixture drops from a spoon as you count to three.

10.

Smooth the icing all over the top and sides of the cake. Let it set before serving.

Serve your Sachertorte with whipped cream.

Sweden, Norway and Finland

Sweden, Norway, Denmark, Finland and Iceland make up Scandinavia. You can find out about Denmark and its food on page 30.

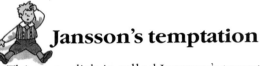

Smörgåsbord

Sweden is most famous for its smörgåsbord, which means 'bread and butter table'. The smörgåsbord is a selection of salads, fish dishes, hot food, desserts and breads laid out on a big table. Here are two typical smörgåsbord dishes.

Jansson's temptation

This tasty dish is called Jansson's temptation. It was probably named after a Swedish opera singer called Pelle Janzon, who loved it.

You will need:

500g/1lb potatoes, peeled
2 large onions, chopped
2 cans anchovies, drained
60g/¼ cup butter

300ml/1 cup milk
pinch salt and pepper

 Set the oven to 200°C (400°F)/ Gas mark 6

Scandinavia is often known as the 'Land of the Midnight Sun'. This is because, during its short summers, the sun shines all day and all night.

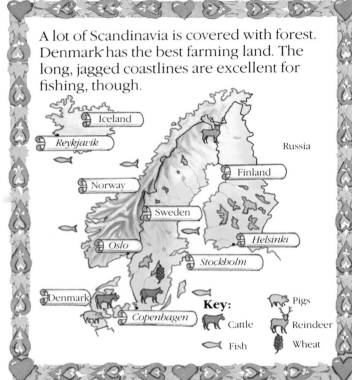

A lot of Scandinavia is covered with forest. Denmark has the best farming land. The long, jagged coastlines are excellent for fishing, though.

Iceland
Reykjavik
Russia
Finland
Norway
Sweden
Helsinki
Oslo
Stockholm
Denmark
Copenhagen

Key:
Cattle
Fish
Pigs
Reindeer
Wheat

1.
Cut the potatoes into thin strips 2cm (1in) wide and 4cm (2ins) long. Put a layer in a small, but deep pie dish.

2.
Cover the potato layer with one of anchovies, then one of chopped onions. Repeat to the top of the dish.

3.
Finish off with a layer of potato strips. Add salt and pepper and pour the milk over the top of it all.

4.
Put small blobs of butter over the dish. Bake it for about 45 minutes, until it is crisp and brown.

Christmas crown

December 13, or St Lucia's Day, is the beginning of Christmas in Sweden. Young girls dress in white, wear a crown of candles and give out cakes and wine.

Red fruit pudding

Poor knights

Fruit ripens quickly in the short Scandinavian summer. People make special fruit puddings, like this, to celebrate Midsummer. This recipe is from Norway.

You will need:

500g/16 oz can of raspberries, blackberries or blueberries

2tbs granulated sugar
2tbs cornstarch
450ml/1½ cups cold water or juice from the canned fruit
some flaked almonds

This recipe for a sweet snack comes from Finland.

You will need:

2 eggs
300ml/1 cup milk
pinch cinnamon
8 slices bread
30g/2 tbs butter
60g/¼ cup granulated sugar

1.

Put the fruit, sugar and water or juice in a pan. Cook over a low heat for five minutes to soften the fruit. Let it cool.

2.

Push the fruit mixture through a sieve into a bowl. Use a metal spoon. Throw away any bits that won't squeeze through.

3.

In a cup, mix the cornstarch with a spoonful of the fruity liquid. Stir this mixture into the fruit.

1.

In a bowl, beat the eggs, milk and cinnamon together. Stir in half the granulated sugar.

Stir it with a wooden spoon all the time.

4.

Pour the fruit mixture back into the pan and bring it to a boil. Lower the heat and cook for five minutes.

5.

When cool, pour the fruit into bowls. Sprinkle with the nuts and chill for 30 minutes in the refrigerator.

2.

Trim the crusts off the bread. Soak the slices in the milk mixture for five minutes.

Fry two or three slices at a time.

3.

Melt the butter in a frying pan. Fry the slices of bread until golden on both sides.

You could serve a pitcher of cream with your fruit pudding.

4.

Sprinkle your poor knights with the rest of the sugar. Serve with jam or fruit and cream.

Denmark

Denmark is part of Scandinavia, but the sea separates it from Norway, Sweden and Finland. It is famous for the bacon and cheese it produces.

These traditional open-faced sandwiches make a tempting, colorful spread for lunch or a snack.

Smørrebrød

Danish open-faced sandwiches are called smørrebrød, which means 'buttered bread' in Danish. To make them, just lay the ingredients onto a slice of buttered bread. Eat them with a knife and fork.

Shrimps and lemon

Put a lettuce leaf on the bread. Spoon on some shrimps. Top with a lemon twist (see below) and black pepper.

Salami and tomato

Cover the bread with overlapping slices of salami. Add two slices of tomato and some onion rings (see below).

Cheese and tomato

Lay slices of cheese on top of the bread. Put a row of overlapping tomato slices up the middle.

Cheese and anchovy

Cover the bread with slices of cheese. Add crisscrossed strips of anchovy and some onion rings (see below).

Lettuce and egg

Put a lettuce leaf on the bread. Cover with overlapping slices of hard-boiled egg and a little parsley.

Twists and twirls

Delicious, sticky cakes are a Danish speciality. Other people call them Danish pastries, but the Danes call them 'Viennese bread'. They come in many shapes and sizes.

Decorating smørrebrød

Here are some ideas for making your smørrebrød colorful and attractive.

1.
Make a small cut up the middle of a slice of lemon. Twist it like this so it stands up.

2.
Slice a pickle lengthwise several times almost down to the end. Spread the slices out like a fan.

3.
You could slice across the top of an onion to make rings. Also try parsley or chopped green onions.

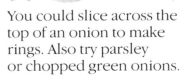

Switzerland

Switzerland is right in the middle of Europe. People speak four different languages, depending on what part of the country they live in. They are French, Italian, German and Romansh.

Raclette

The two best-known Swiss cheeses are called Emmental and Gruyère. Traditionally, people held the whole cheese on a fork in front of a fire to melt some for this dish. It's easier to melt slices of cheese under a broiler, though.

You will need:

4 medium potatoes
250g/8oz cheese
(preferably Swiss)

The Alps mountains cover most of Switzerland. Cows graze on the grassy slopes. They produce the creamy milk that makes Swiss chocolate and cheese.

France Germany **Key**
Zurich 🐄 Cattle
Berne Austria
Geneva
Italy

1.

Scrub the potatoes, but do not peel them. Boil them until a knife comes out easily when stuck in (about 15 minutes).

2.

Cut the potatoes in half lengthwise. Lay slices of cheese over the flat side and broil them until the cheese melts.

Swiss people serve raclette with pickled onions.

Children eat raclette in a famous Swiss children's book, called 'Heidi'.

Muesli

Muesli is a mixture of grains, such as oats, with fruit and nuts. It was first made in 1897 by a Swiss doctor called Bircher-Brenner, as a healthy breakfast food. Change the amounts of each ingredient to suit your taste.

The word muesli comes from the German word muësli, which means 'mixture'.

For each person:

1 tbs rolled oats
1 tbs wheat flakes
1 tbs barley flakes
6 tbs water
1 tbs chopped mixed nuts
1 tbs dried fruit
2 tbs lemon juice
1 apple
1 tbs honey
milk

1.

In a bowl, soak the oats, wheat and barley in the water before you go to bed at night. This will soften them.

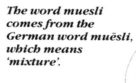

2.

In the morning, peel and grate the apple. Add lemon juice to keep it from turning brown. Stir it into the soaked grains.

3.

Add the dried fruit and as much milk as you want. Top with the spoonful of honey and the nuts.

Greece and Turkey

People eat similar sorts of food in Greece and Turkey, but both countries have specialities. Some of them, such as kebabs, are popular in many countries today. Some traditional recipes were first written down over 2,000 years ago, by the Ancient Greeks.

Shish kebabs

In this Turkish recipe, cubes of lamb are cooked on metal skewers to make shish kebabs. This means 'roast meat stuck on a skewer'. Serve them in pita bread with salad. This recipe makes eight kebabs.

Watch the sharp skewer.

1. Mix the oil, 3 tbs of the lemon juice, oregano, salt and pepper in a glass bowl. Soak the meat cubes in this mixture for one hour.

2. Wash the lettuce and dry it with a paper towel. Cut the leaves into strips. Cut the tomatoes into quarters and slice the cucumber.

3. Push about six cubes of meat onto each skewer. Leave a little gap between each cube. Sprinkle them with a little rosemary.

You will need:

750g/1½lbs lamb, cut into cubes
4 tbs olive oil
4 tbs lemon juice
½ tsp oregano
½ tsp rosemary
pinch salt and pepper
8 lettuce leaves
4 tomatoes
½ a cucumber
8 pita breads

Wear oven mitts. The skewers will be hot.

4. Broil the kebabs under a hot broiler for about 10 minutes. Keep turning them to make sure they cook all the way through.

5. Warm the pita breads quickly under the broiler. Carefully slice each one along the top and open it up, like an envelope.

6. Put some salad into each pita. Push the meat cubes off a skewer into each one. Sprinkle with the rest of the lemon juice.

Cakes and sweets

Greek and Turkish cakes and sweets are very sweet. Special cake shops sell them.

This is Turkish delight. It is made by boiling grapes into a jelly. Sometimes it is flavored with roses.

This is a baklava. It is made of thin pastry called filo. It is filled with nuts, then soaked in honey.

This cake, called a kadeifi, is made from pastry that looks a bit like cotton yarn. People often eat it with coffee.

You could serve your kebabs with rice instead of in pita.

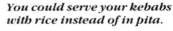

Moussaka

This delicious Greek dish traditionally uses minced lamb. You can use beef, though. If you are vegetarian, try a mixture of tomatoes, onions, zucchini and mushrooms instead.

You will need:

1 large eggplant	*pinch oregano*
500g/1lb ground lamb	*pinch salt and pepper*
1 large onion, chopped	*30g/2 tbs butter*
4 tbs olive oil	*1 tbs flour*
1 16 oz can tomatoes	*1 egg*
	300ml/1 cup milk
	60g/¼ cup grated parmesan cheese

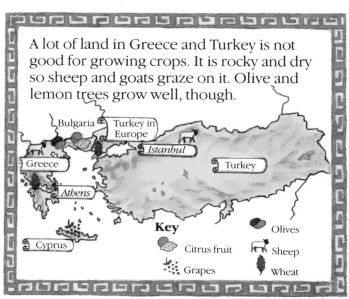

A lot of land in Greece and Turkey is not good for growing crops. It is rocky and dry so sheep and goats graze on it. Olive and lemon trees grow well, though.

Key
Olives
Citrus fruit
Sheep
Grapes
Wheat

Set the oven to 190°C(375°F)/ Gas mark 5

Put the lid on to cook.

1.
Slice the eggplant into 1cm (½in) slices. Heat 2 tbs of oil in a pan with a lid. Fry the onion and meat until browned. Add the tomatoes, oregano, salt and pepper. Cook for 30 minutes.

2.
In a frying pan, heat the rest of the oil and fry each slice of eggplant until it is soft. Then flip it over and cook the other side. Do a few slices at a time. Add more oil if you need to.

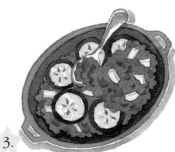

3.
Spoon half of the meat mixture into a casserole (deep, ovenproof dish). Cover it with a layer of eggplant slices. Repeat the layers with the rest of the meat and eggplants.

In Greece, this cheese is often added to salads. It is called feta.

4.
In a small bowl, beat the egg. Melt the butter in a pan. Stir in the flour to make a smooth paste. Cook it for one minute. Keep stirring.

Stir the whole time.

5.
Remove from heat and stir in milk. Return to medium heat and bring to boil, stirring constantly. Remove from heat. Add some mixture to the beaten egg and stir into sauce.

6.
Pour the sauce over the casserole. Sprinkle your moussaka with the grated cheese and cook it in the oven for about 45 minutes, until it is brown and crisp on top. Serve it hot with a fresh salad.

Tasty tavernas

In Greece and Turkey, people often eat in restaurants called tavernas. Many are outside, with shady vines instead of solid roofs.

The Middle East

The area called the Middle East stretches from the top of Africa in the west across to the edge of the former Soviet Union in the east. It includes 20 separate countries. Most people in Middle Eastern countries are Muslim, so they do not eat pork or drink alcohol. Families usually eat meals together, though it is traditional for people not to speak at all while they are eating.

Mezze

Many Middle Eastern meals begin with a selection of appetizers, which are called 'mezze'. Health food stores sell all the ingredients you need.

Homous

This chickpea paste is called homous. It makes a good snack or a tasty appetizer.

You will need:

250g/1 cup dried chick-peas, soaked in water overnight, or
1 16 oz can chickpeas
1 clove of garlic, peeled and crushed
1 tbs light tahina (sesame seed paste)

6 tbs lemon juice
2 tbs olive oil
3 tbs milk
pinch salt and pepper

To decorate:
a sprig of fresh parsley

A lot of the Middle East is desert. Farmers grow fruit and vegetables such as chickpeas and lentils where enough rain falls. They keep sheep and goats, too.

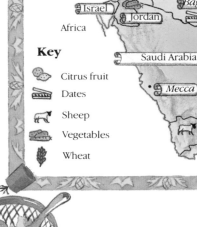

Russia
Turkey
Lebanon Beirut Iraq Tehran
Tel Aviv Jerusalem Iran
Israel Baghdad
Africa Jordan
Saudi Arabia
Mecca
Oman
Yemen

Key
Citrus fruit
Dates
Sheep
Vegetables
Wheat

Keep an eye on the boiling chickpeas. Add more water if they dry up.

1.

Boil fresh chickpeas in water for two hours, or until soft. Drain the water and let them cool. If you are using canned ones, just pour out the water.

2.

Put four whole chickpeas aside. Put the rest into a blender, or push them through a sieve with a spoon. They will make a smooth paste.

Tasty tea

Middle Eastern people shop in indoor markets called souks. In tiny tea shops, they can refresh themselves with glasses of mint tea.

3.

Mix in all the other ingredients. Put the whole chickpeas and the parsley on top. Serve your homous with some warmed pita bread (you need to buy this).

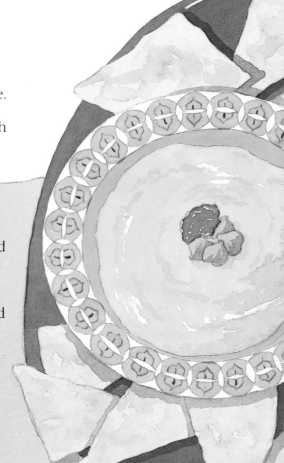

Tabouli

This crunchy salad comes from Lebanon. It can be a snack or an appetizer (mezze). It uses a grain called bulgur. People in the Middle East scoop it up with lettuce leaves to eat it.

You will need:

250g/8oz fine bulgur
6 green onions
3 tomatoes
1 green pepper
4 lettuce leaves

2 sprigs each chopped fresh parsley and mint or 2 tbs each if dried
6 tbs olive oil
6 tbs lemon juice
pinch salt and pepper

The spoon squeezes the water out of the grains.

1. Soak the bulgur in cold water for 15 minutes. Pour it into a sieve and push down with a spoon.

2. Chop the green onions and tomatoes. Cut out the pepper's core and seeds and chop it into small pieces.

Dry the lettuce on a tea towel or paper towels.

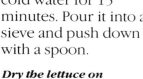

3. Wash the lettuce leaves and pat them dry. In a small bowl, mix the oil, lemon juice, salt and pepper together.

4. In a big bowl, mix up the bulgur, vegetables, parsley and mint. Add the oil mixture and stir everything well.

5. Put a lettuce leaf on each person's plate. Pile some tabouli on top and serve.

Halva

Halva is a type of candy. There are many different types. A square of halva is often served at the end of a meal in the Middle East, with glasses of tea or strong coffee.

You will need:

90g/1/3 cup granulated sugar
120g/1/2 cup butter
120g/4oz semolina
300ml/1 cup water
1 tsp vanilla

To decorate: about 20 blanched almonds (without their brown skins)

1. Cook the sugar and water over a low heat until the sugar is dissolved. The water will turn clear.

Keep stirring all the time.

2. Melt the butter in another pan. Add the semolina and cook for three minutes. Stir all the time. Add the vanilla.

3. Remove from heat, stir the sugary water into the semolina. Return to the heat, stir for three more minutes, until very thick.

4. Pour it into a dish 25cm (10in) across and 1cm (1/2in) deep. Smooth the top and score 5cm (2in) squares.

5. Stick an almond in the middle of each square. Serve squares of cool halva with tea or coffee.

Russia

Russia is the biggest of the republics, or states, that made up what used to be called the Soviet Union. Together, they cover an area bigger than all of Europe. They all have their own cooking traditions, but while they were united some recipes became popular throughout the region.

Russian salad

Vegetables are used to make all types of dishes in Russia. Here, they are cooked and made into a crunchy salad. Serve it as an appetizer, or as a meal in itself. You can add some cheese, ham or tuna if you like.

You will need:

2 medium carrots
3 medium potatoes
90g/³⁄4 cup peas (cooked frozen peas or canned peas)
3 small cooked beets
2 tbs mayonnaise
pinch salt and pepper
washed lettuce leaves to line the salad bowl
10 slices cucumber
1 hard-boiled egg
(see page 16)

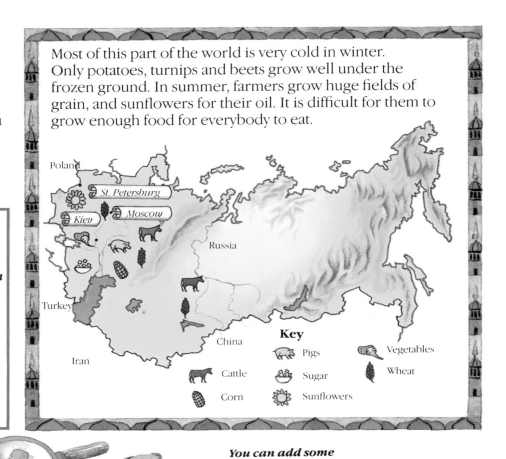

Most of this part of the world is very cold in winter. Only potatoes, turnips and beets grow well under the frozen ground. In summer, farmers grow huge fields of grain, and sunflowers for their oil. It is difficult for them to grow enough food for everybody to eat.

Poland
St. Petersburg
Kiev   Moscow
Russia
Turkey
China
Iran

Key
Pigs   Vegetables
Cattle   Sugar   Wheat
Corn   Sunflowers

1.
Peel the potatoes and carrots. Cook them for 15 minutes in a pan of boiling water with the lid on.

2.
Pour the water off the vegetables and let them cool. Line a small dish with the washed lettuce leaves.

3.
Chop the vegetables and beets into 1cm (½in) cubes. Pour them into a bowl. Add the peas, salt and pepper.

4.
Stir the mayonnaise into the vegetables. Spoon them into the dish. Decorate with slices of cucumber and hard-boiled egg.

You can add some chopped cooked chicken or fish to your Russian salad if you like.

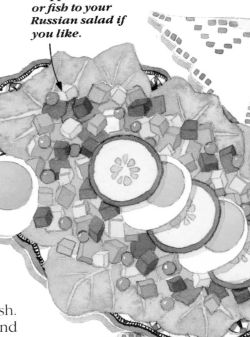

Easter eggs

In some places, children dye and decorate hard-boiled eggs to celebrate Easter. If you want to try it, you can buy egg dyes from craft shops or make your own with some of these vegetables.

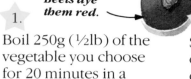

Spinach dyes eggs green.

Onions give a rich brown.

Beets dye them red.

These are some traditional Russian egg-patterns.

1.
Boil 250g (½lb) of the vegetable you choose for 20 minutes in a large pan of water. The water will change color.

2.
Spoon the vegetables out of the pan. Boil the eggs in the colored water in the pan for ten minutes.

3.
Let the eggs cool. Dip a toothpick stick in vinegar or lemon juice and scratch a pattern onto the dyed egg.

Beef Stroganoff

This recipe was first made in the 1700's, for Count Alexander Stroganoff. You need expensive steak to cook it properly, so save it for special occasions.

You will need:

500g/1lb sirloin steak
60g/4 tbs butter
1 medium onion, sliced
120g/1 cup mushrooms, sliced

150ml/½ cup sour cream
1 tsp Dijon mustard
1 tsp salt and pepper
16 oz beef bouillon

1.
On a board, cut the steak into strips about 1cm (½in) wide and 6cm (2½ins) long. Sprinkle them with salt and pepper and cover with paper towels.

2.
Melt the butter in a large frying pan. Add the onion slices and fry them until they are soft and see-through. Keep stirring them all the time.

3.
Add the sliced mushrooms and fry them for about two minutes. Stir in the mustard. Carefully lay the strips of steak around the frying pan. Watch your fingers.

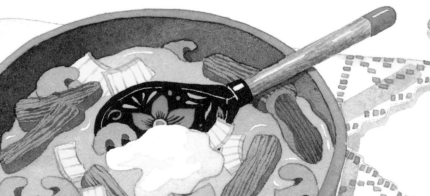

4.
Cook your Stroganoff for about five minutes, moving the ingredients around the frying pan all the time. The steak will turn brown on both sides.

5.
Turn the heat down, add the bouillon and stir in the sour cream. Cook gently for another two minutes, then serve right away with rice or flat noodles.

China

Chinese food is popular in many countries today. There are thousands of different Chinese dishes. Some more unusual recipes use ingredients such as chickens' feet, sharks' fins and birds' nests. But most Chinese people cook simpler dishes like the ones on this page.

Sweet and sour spare ribs

Chinese recipes often combine different tastes, such as sweet and sour. This sauce adds a tangy taste to pork spare ribs.

You will need:

1.5kg/3lbs meaty pork spare ribs
1 small onion, chopped
1 clove of garlic, peeled and crushed
1 tbs grated fresh ginger, or 1 tsp dried ginger

3 tbs vegetable oil
pinch salt
2 tbs sugar
2 tbs vinegar
1 tbs soy sauce
1½ tbs tomato paste
2 tbs orange juice

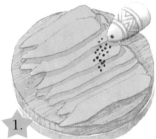

1.
Rinse and pat dry the spare ribs. Cut off as much of the fat as you can. Sprinkle them with a little salt.

2.
Pour the sugar, vinegar, soy sauce, tomato paste and orange juice into a deep casserole dish. Stir them well.

3.
Put the ribs in the sauce, cover and leave them for about an hour. They will soak up the flavors in the sauce.

4.
Heat the oil in a frying pan. Fry the ribs for about five minutes, stirring them all the time as they cook.

⚠️ *Cook your ribs a few at a time. Keep them warm in a low oven.*

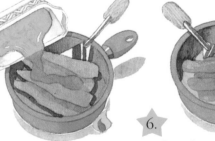

5.
Turn the heat down a bit and add the onion, garlic, ginger and the sauce from the casserole dish.

6.
Fry for about ten more minutes, until the pork is crisp. Keep stirring the ribs around the pan so that they do not burn.

7.
Lift the ribs onto plates and spoon the sauce in the pan over them. It's best to eat them with your fingers.

You could serve spare-ribs as an appetizer, or with some rice as a main course.

Stir-frying
Chinese food is often fried over a high heat in a pan called a wok. The first woks were used over 5,000 years ago in China. Food is stirred all the time, so this way of cooking is called stir-frying.

Fried rice with vegetables

Chinese people cook rice in lots of different ways. For this recipe, you need to cook it as the packet tells you before you start.

China is huge and over a billion people live there. Farmers plant rice, wheat and maize. They also keep cattle, pigs, chickens and ducks for their meat.

Russia

India

Peking

Shanghai

Hong Kong

Key

Cattle

Citrus fruit

Ducks   Rice

Fish   Pigs

Maize   Wheat

You will need:

375g/4 cups cooked rice
6 mushrooms
150g/1 cup bean sprouts
6 iceberg lettuce leaves or Chinese leaves, if you can get them
120g/1 cup frozen peas

6 green onions
1 garlic clove, peeled and crushed
1 tsp grated fresh ginger or 2 tsps, if dried
3 tbs soy sauce
3 tbs vegetable oil (groundnut or sesame oil is best)

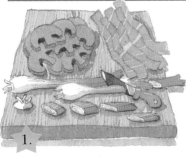

1.

Slice the mushrooms. Cut the lettuce leaves into thin strips. Slice the green onions into 2cm (1in) slices with your knife at a slant.

2. ⚠

In a frying pan, heat the oil until a haze rises. Add the garlic and ginger and fry for 30 seconds. Stir them all the time.

3.

Add the mushrooms and fry for two minutes. Stir in the green onions, peas, lettuce, rice and bean sprouts. Keep everything moving.

4.

Sprinkle on the soy sauce and stir-fry (fry and stir all the time) for five more minutes. If the rice starts to stick, add 2 tbs of water. Serve at once.

You can add pieces of cooked shrimps, chicken or tuna to fried rice at step 3, if you like.

How to use chopsticks

Chinese people eat with chopsticks. If you want to try using them, you might find it tricky at first, so keep practicing.

Slide the thick end of one chopstick in the hollow between your thumb and first finger.

Rest the middle firmly on your third finger.

Hold the second chopstick between your thumb and your first finger, as you would hold a pen.

Move your first finger and thumb to lift the top chopstick up and down. The ends will pinch together to pick up food.

India

Cooking styles in India are very different from one area to another. What people can cook and eat depends on their religion, too. Indian cooks are expert at blending spices to create delicious flavors in their dishes.

Over 300 million people live in India. Growing enough food is difficult, so most land has to be farmed in some way. Grain, rice, tea and spices are the main crops.

Thali

Most Indian meals are made up of several dishes. Often, each dish is served in a small metal bowl called a 'katori'. The katoris are all laid on a tray called a 'thali', so meals like this are called 'thalis', too. Rice is usually put in the middle.

Bhuna gosht

Indians do not use the word curry. People from the West gave Indian dishes this name. The mixture of spices makes each Indian dish different. This one is made of lamb and tomatoes.

You will need:

750g/1½lbs lean lamb
1 onion, chopped
2 cloves garlic, peeled and crushed
60g/4 tbs butter
3 tomatoes, quartered
1 16 oz can tomatoes
4 tbs lemon juice
bouillon cube
plus 300ml/1 cup boiling water
pinch salt
1 tsp chili powder
2 tsp ground coriander
2 tsp black pepper
1 tsp ground cumin
1 tsp turmeric

Basmati rice

The best rice for Indian dishes is basmati rice. Cook about 60g/2oz of rice for each person. Follow the instructions on the packet or box.

1. Melt the butter in a frying pan. Fry the onion and garlic for about five minutes, until they are soft.

2. Cut the lamb into 2.5cm (1in) cubes. In a bowl, sprinkle them with salt and lemon juice. Let them soak for 15 minutes.

3. Stir the spices, pepper, onion and garlic into the lamb. Add the tomatoes and pour into a deep pan.

4. Dissolve the bouillon cube in the boiling water and add it to the pan. Let your bhuna gosht bubble gently for an hour.

5. Taste your bhuna and stir in a little more chili powder if you like spicy food. Serve hot with some rice.

Dhal

Dhal is the Indian word for pulse vegetables such as lentils and beans. Over 50 different sorts of dhal grow in India. Cooks make them into a spicy sauce, which is also called a dhal.

Wash the lentils and pick out any stones.

Add more water if they start to stick.

1. Melt the butter in a deep pan. Fry the garlic and onion for about three minutes, until they are soft.

2. Add the turmeric, chili powder, lentils and water. Bring to a boil, stirring all the time.

3. Turn the heat down and let the mixture bubble for about 20 minutes. The lentils will turn soft and mushy.

4. Remove from heat, stir in the salt. Pour your dhal into a serving bowl and sprinkle with a little ground cumin.

Cucumber raita

Raitas are made of yogurt mixed with fresh vegetables and herbs. They cool your mouth after spicier dishes.

Black pepper

1. Peel the cucumber and slice it lengthwise, from top to bottom. Now cut the slices into strips about 3cms (1½ins) long.

2. Mix the cucumber strips with all the other ingredients in a bowl. Cover with cling wrap and put in the refrigerator for 30 minutes.

Making masalas

The mixture of freshly-ground herbs and spices in an Indian dish is called a masala. Curry powder is a ready-made masala, but it is not as good as a fresh one.

This is turmeric. It colors food yellow and adds a spicy flavor.

These cumin seeds have a strong, scented taste.

Coriander adds a delicate perfume as well as taste.

Mustard seeds add hot, peppery flavor to any dish.

These are cardamom pods. They have a fresh taste.

Chili powder

Black pepper

Ginger

Black pepper, ginger, cloves, nutmeg and chilis go into masalas, too.

Nutmeg

Cloves

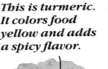

Japan

Food in Japan is some of the healthiest in the world. It is beautifully presented as well. The Japanese eat a lot of fish, vegetables, noodles and rice. It can be difficult to get exactly the right Japanese ingredients, such as dried seaweed and fish. The ones suggested here give you a taste of their cooking. Health food stores sell all the things you need to make this meal.

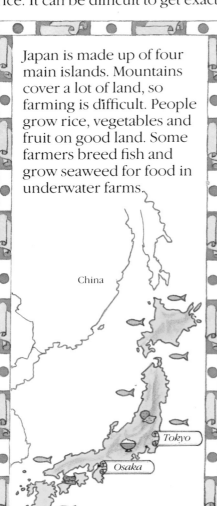

Japan is made up of four main islands. Mountains cover a lot of land, so farming is difficult. People grow rice, vegetables and fruit on good land. Some farmers breed fish and grow seaweed for food in underwater farms.

China

Tokyo

Osaka

Key

🐟 Fish

🍚 Rice

🍊 Citrus fruit

🥬 Vegetables

Vegetable casserole

Traditionally, people make this dish in the winter in Japan. Arrange the vegetables attractively in the dish to look really Japanese.

You will need:

3 medium carrots	*1 chicken bouillon cube*	*120g/4oz rice noodles*
4 green onions	*600ml/2 cups boiling water*	
4 mushrooms		
3 cabbage leaves	*2 tsp soy sauce*	
1 medium potato	*2 tbs brown sugar*	*Set the oven to 170°C(325°F)/ Gas mark 3*
150g/5oz tofu (soya bean curd)	*pinch salt*	

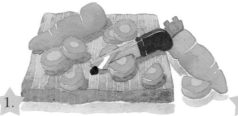

1. Peel the carrots. Cut them into slices about ½cm (¼in) thick. Then cut each slice in half.

2. Cut the ends off the green onions. Slanting your knife, cut them into 4cm (2in) sections.

3. Wipe the mushrooms with damp paper towels. Trim the stems and cut a cross in the tops.

Wedge of leaves

4. Roll up the cabbage leaves and slice through each to make wedges of leaves.

5. Peel the potato. Cut it into slices ½cm (¼in) thick. Cut the tofu into 2cm (1in) cubes.

6. Dissolve the bouillon cube in the boiling water Stir in the soy sauce, sugar and salt.

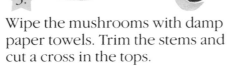

7. Arrange each vegetable in a group around a casserole dish. Add the noodles in a group too.

8. Pour on the broth and cook your casserole with the lid on for about 45 minutes.

Japanese meals

The dishes of a Japanese meal are all put onto a low table at the same time. People sit on cushions on the floor to eat with chopsticks. (See how to use them on page 39).

Sushi snacks

Sushi is raw fish and rice, often wrapped in dried seaweed. Sushi is served as an appetizer or as a carryout snack from cafés in Japan called 'sushi bars'. Sushi chefs train for years to make it exactly the right way.

 ## Rice

In Japan, rice is so important that the Japanese word for rice, 'gohan', also means food. Cook about 60g (2oz) of long grain rice for each person. Follow the instructions on the packet.

There is often a stylish flower arrangement on Japanese tables. Making them is an ancient art called 'ikebana'.

Dipping sauce

The Japanese often dip each piece of food from the main dish in a dipping sauce before they eat it. These sauces are put in a tiny bowl next to a person's chopsticks and eating bowl.

You will need:

6 tbs lemon juice
6 tbs soy sauce
1 tbs brown sugar

Mix the ingredients together in a bowl. Put the sauce in the refrigerator for as long as you can before pouring into saucers and serving it with your Japanese meal.

Set the table very simply, without cluttering it up. Each person needs a bowl and a spoon or chopsticks.

The art of arranging food is called 'moritsuke' in Japan.

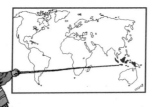

Indonesia

Indonesia is made up of over 3,000 islands. They are famous for the spices that grow there. For centuries, people called them The Spice Islands.

Chicken in coconut sauce

More coconuts grow in Indonesia than anywhere else in the world, so cooks there use them a lot. They add a creamy taste to this chicken dish. Try serving it with plain boiled rice.

You will need:

4 chicken breasts
3 tbs vegetable oil
2 onions, chopped
3 cloves of garlic, peeled and crushed

60g/2oz cream of coconut (most supermarkets sell it)
300ml/1 cup hot water
1 tbs lemon juice
1 tsp ground ginger
1 tsp chili powder
pinch salt and pepper

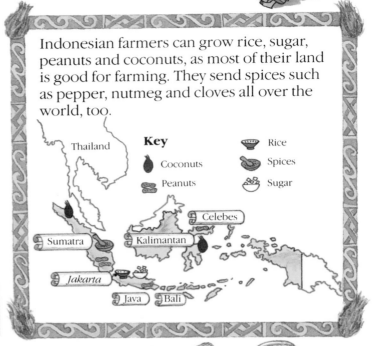

Indonesian farmers can grow rice, sugar, peanuts and coconuts, as most of their land is good for farming. They send spices such as pepper, nutmeg and cloves all over the world, too.

Key

Thailand

Coconuts · Rice
Peanuts · Spices · Sugar

Celebes
Sumatra · Kalimantan
Jakarta
Java · Bali

1.
Heat the oil in a large frying pan. Gently lower the chicken breasts into it. Cook them for about five minutes on each side.

2.
Lift the chicken breasts out onto some paper towels. Sprinkle them with the ginger, chili powder, salt, pepper and lemon juice.

3.
Fry the onions and garlic until they are soft. In a bowl, dissolve the creamed coconut in the hot water to make a thin, white milk.

4.
Put the chicken back into the pan and pour the coconut milk over the top. Cook the dish over a low heat for about 40 minutes.

Indonesian food is often beautifully presented. Try decorating your dish with a sprig of mint or a wedge of lemon.

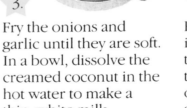

Smelly fruit

This fruit, called the durian fruit, is very popular in Indonesia. It smells like rotten cheese but tastes like sweet custard, people say.

Australia and New Zealand

The original people in Australia were called Aborigines, and Maoris first lived in New Zealand. In the 1700's, European convicts were sent there, far from home, as a punishment. They planted crops from Europe, and cooking here is now a mixture of traditional and European styles.

Lamingtons

These cakes were named after an Australian politician called Bruce Lamington. They are now popular in Australia and New Zealand.

You will need:

250g/1 cup butter or margarine
180g/²/₃ cup granulated sugar
250g/1½ cups self-rising flour
2 eggs
6 tbs milk
1 tsp vanilla

120g/4oz powdered sugar
1 tbs cocoa
2 tbs warm water
90g/1¼ cups toasted coconut

Set the oven to 170°C (325°F)/ Gas mark 3

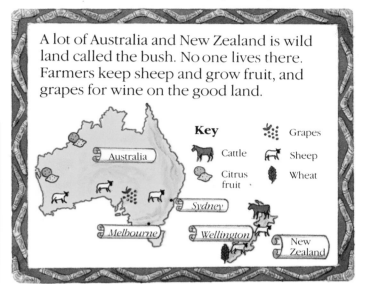

A lot of Australia and New Zealand is wild land called the bush. No one lives there. Farmers keep sheep and grow fruit, and grapes for wine on the good land.

Key
Grapes
Cattle
Sheep
Citrus fruit
Wheat

Australia
Sydney
Melbourne
Wellington
New Zealand

Put the butter and sugar in a bowl. Use a wooden spoon to mix them together until they are smooth and creamy.

In another bowl, whisk the eggs with a fork. Beat them into the butter mixture gradually. Stir in the milk and vanilla.

Beach barbecue

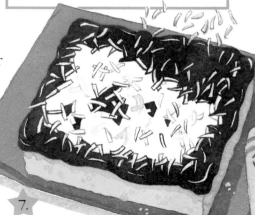

Barbecues are a speciality of Australia and New Zealand. The sunny climate is ideal for cooking outside. Christmas Day there is in mid summer, so Christmas lunch is often a barbecue on the beach.

3.

Sift the flour into a bowl. Add it to the mixture by making gentle slicing movements with a metal spoon. Stir gently.

4.

Use a pan 18 x 28cm (7 x 11in) and 4cm (1½in) deep.

Grease and line a baking pan. Pour in the mixture and smooth the top. Bake for 25-30 minutes, until golden brown.

5.

Let the cake cool, then cut it into 7cm (3in) squares. Lift each square out onto a wire rack to cool down.

6.

Sift the powdered sugar and cocoa into a bowl. Mix in the water for a smooth, runny paste that drops from a spoon as you count to three.

7.

Using a metal spoon, spread icing onto the top of each square. Let it drip down the sides. Sprinkle with coconut.

Jewish cooking

Jewish people live in many countries of the world. Their religion has strict laws about how food is prepared. When cooks follow these rules, the food they make is called kosher, which means 'suitable'. Jewish recipes vary slightly from country to country, as cooks adapt them to what food is available. You do not need to be Jewish, or know their rules, to enjoy these two dishes.

Cheesecake

Jewish cheesecake is usually baked in an oven, cooled, then chilled in a refrigerator. It takes a bit of time to make, but is a delicious dessert.

You will need:

10 graham crackers
90g/5 tbs butter or margarine
375g/12oz cream cheese or curd cheese
3 eggs, separated (see page 5)
90g/½ cup granulated sugar

6 tbs lemon juice
150ml/½ cup heavy cream

 Set the oven to 180°C(350°F)/Gas mark 4

Springform pan

1. Put the graham crackers into a clean plastic bag. Roll a rolling pin over the bag until the graham crackers are crumbs.

2. Melt the butter in a pan. Remove from heat, stir in the crumbs. Make sure the butter is well mixed in.

3. Pour the mixture into a 20cm (8in) greased springform pan. Press it flat with the back of a spoon. Bake it for ten minutes.

4. Beat together the cheese and egg yolks. Add the sugar, cream and lemon juice and beat again.

This takes a few minutes.

A long wait

Cheesecake reminds Jews of their prophet Moses, they say. He waited so long for God to tell him the rules of their faith that milk had time to turn into cheese.

5. Whisk the egg whites until they form soft peaks.

6. Making cutting movements with a metal spoon, gently add the egg whites to the creamy mixture.

7. Pour the mixture into the crumb crust and cook for 45-50 minutes until firm. Refrigerate for one hour before removing the outside of the pan.

Potato latkes

These crispy potato cakes are called latkes. They are delicious hot, right after cooking, or served cold with some sour cream and salad. This recipe makes ten latkes.

You will need:

4 medium-sized potatoes
1 small onion

1 egg
pinch salt and pepper
3 tbs vegetable oil

The water keeps it from turning brown.

1.

Peel and then grate the potatoes. Put the grated potato into a bowl of cold water right away.

2.

Peel and grate the onion. In a bowl, beat the egg with a fork. Add the onion, salt and pepper and beat again.

3.

Pour the grated potato into a sieve and shake off any water. Add it to the egg mixture and stir well.

4.

Heat the oil in a frying pan. Put tablespoonfuls of mixture into the pan and press them flat.

5.

Fry each latke for about five minutes on each side. Lift them onto paper towels and serve right away.

Jewish bread

In most countries where Jews live, shops sell kosher food for them to eat. Jewish bakeries sell several sorts of kosher bread, cakes and wafers. Here are three of them.

This is a bagel. Bagels are delicious served sliced in half and filled with smoked salmon and cream cheese.

This plaited bread is called challah. It is baked specially for Jewish festivals.

These wafers are called matzos. They are often crumbled into soups or made into dumplings called matzo balls.

Index

The words which appear in *italics* are things which you can buy as part of a meal. They are not things to make.

First published in America August 1993 **AE**

First published in 1992 by Usborne Publishing Ltd, Usborne House, 83-85 Saffron Hill, London EC1N 8RT, England. Copyright © Usborne Publishing Ltd, 1992. The name Usborne and the device 🎈 are Trade Marks of Usborne Publishing Ltd. All rights reserved.